GHOST TOWN
BOTTLE PRICE GUIDE

GHOST TOWN
BOTTLE PRICE GUIDE

AVERAGE MARKET PRICE GUIDE FOR ANTIQUE
BOTTLE COLLECTORS,

WITH AN EXPANDED SECTION
ON ORIENTAL RELICS

By
WES and RUBY BRESSIE

Illustrations
By
JEANNE BRESSIE

Photos
By
TERRY SKIBBY

8th Edition, Revised and Enlarged

The CAXTON PRINTERS, Ltd.
Caldwell
1973

First printing May, 1972
Second printing June, 1973

ISBN 0-87004-225-4
Library of Congress Card Catalog No. 79-151058

Printed in the United States of America by
The CAXTON PRINTERS, Ltd.
Caldwell, Idaho
121801

Dedicated to all bottle collectors who see a hidden beauty and a part of western history unveiled in an old bottle.

TABLE OF CONTENTS

LIST OF ILLUSTRATIONS

INTRODUCTION

Within the past few years, a tremendous interest has grown up around the collecting of antique bottles. The numbers devoted to this exciting hobby have mushroomed from a handful of collectors to many thousands. Under the strain and tension of modern day living, more people are looking to the outdoors for their recreation. This hobby offers the whole family a chance to enjoy it together. The enjoyment derived from finding an old bottle and realizing the historical significance attached, as well as the possible monetary value of the find, are hearty rewards for the collector.

It is with the monetary value in mind that this revised and enlarged price guide has been compiled. Antique dealers and collectors from several western states have contributed invaluable information, and grateful acknowledgment is extended for their help.

Variations in bottle prices have been noted from different areas, making it doubly hard to come up with an average figure. Although a certain bottle might be rare in one place, in another quantities of the same item might be found, significantly lowering the going rate. None of the bottles listed in this guide has been machine-made, a fact which guarantees a field of the unique and rare alone.

Many antiques have been found in the hunt for old bottles—coins, firearms, and rare china, for instance. In view of these side benefits, an enlarged section on oriental relics which can be found throughout the West has been included for the first time.

Bottles, coins, an old iron cooking pot and a powder horn are a few of the things that have been found while searching for old bottles. The coins and bottles were found at the old Oregon Belle Mine cook shack near Jacksonville, Oregon. The two dimes are Barber or Liberty Head 1896–S and 1898. The half dollar is a Barber, 1892.

This little boy bottle was found at a depth of 10 feet in the Virginia City, Nevada, dump. The colors are still bright. It is possibly a "snort" bottle, similar to the Champaigne Girl. Very rare!

GHOST TOWN BOTTLES

WHISKIES — WINES — BEERS, ETC.

Kellogg's Nelson County
Extra Kentucky Bourbon
Whiskey — W. L. Co.
(opposite side)
Amber, inside threads
$15.00—20.00

Manhattan Club Pure Rye
Whiskey
Brown, squat, 9¾ in. tall
$30.00—40.00

F. Zimmerman & Co.,
Portland, Oregon
Purple or amber, 12 in. tall
$9.00—22.00

Spruance Stanley & Co.
(on horseshoe)
Amber, 11¾ in. tall
$25.00—35.00

Unmarked
Green, squat, with crescent
on shoulder; whittle mold;
7½ in. tall
$10.00—12.00

Pepper Distillery Hand
Made Sour Mash
Dark amber, 11¾ in. tall
$20.00—25.00

J. H. Cutter Old Bourbon —
Cutter O.K. Whiskey (in
circle) — A. P. Hotaling's
O.K. Cutter Whiskey (on
reverse)
Dark amber
$30.00—35.00

> Bouvier's Buchu Gin,
> Louisville, Ky.
> Purple, square, fluted
> shoulders and neck
> **$12.00—15.00**

C. H. Moore Old Bourbon
& Rye — Jesse Moore —
Hunt Co., San Francisco,
(around base)
Trademark located inside
antlers on shoulder
$10.00—20.00

> The F. Chevalier Co. Old
> Castle Whiskey
> Castle in bas relief. Stopper
> reads: "F. Chevalier & Co.";
> has an embossed castle under
> which is Riley's patent
> Amber, inside threads, 11½
> in. tall
> **$12.00—15.00**

Americus Club Pure
Whiskey
Purple, square, swirled
neck, 9½ in. tall
$9.00—12.00

> S. Hirsch & Co. Crystal Brook
> Purple flask, with embossing
> on neck and shoulders
> (Miniature of this is round)
> **$10.00—12.00**

Kellerstrass Distilling
Co.
Purple, fluted shoulders,
12 in. tall
$10.00—12.00

> Unmarked (Oriental Herb
> Bitters)
> Amber, square, sheared lip
> 8 in. tall
> **$25.00—30.00**

A. M. Jones Distillery
No. 97
Distillery was established
in 1881
Dark amber, 10¼ in.
tall
$12.00—18.00

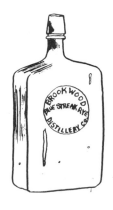

> Brookwood Distillery Co.
> Blue Streak Rye
> Red amber, flat, square,
> 9½ in. tall
> **$10.00—12.00**

Dodson's Extra Special
Brown, rectangular, 11
in. tall
$8.00—10.00

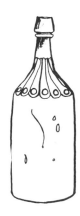

> Unmarked (Whisky)
> Brown, with large dots
> around shoulders; 11 in. tall
> **$4.00—6.00**

Booth & Co., Sacramento
Light purple, embossed
anchor, 12 in. tall
$25.00—35.00

The A. P. Hotaling Co. of
Portland, Ore. – A. P. H.
Co. (on reverse)
Light amber, 12 in. tall
$75.00—125.00

Unmarked (Whisky)
Brown, plain. Fancy em-
bossing on neck and
shoulders; 11 in. tall
$4.00—6.00

Hayner Distilling Co., St.
Louis, Mo., (et. al.)
Hayner's has several variants
Dark amber
$8.00—10.00

Phoenix Bourbon – Naber,
Alfs & Brune – San Francisco
Honey amber
$35.00—40.00

Unmarked
Amber, square; fluting
around neck and shoulders
$3.00—4.00

Flask
Clear, horseshoe-shaped,
embossed with G.D.
Sheared lip, rough base
Rare!
$??

Flask
Brown, bulbous neck,
6¾ in. tall
$3.00—4.00

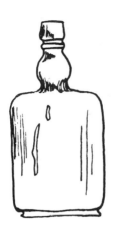

Warranted Flask
Purple
$6.00—8.00

Flask
Sunburst punkin seed,
with embossed clock
Purple, pint
$18.00—20.00

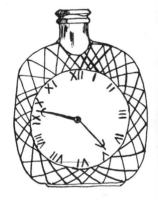

Brown — Forman Co.
Clear flask, 6 in.
tall
$5.00—6.00

Flask
Punkin seed with white
porcelain and wire
stopper. (Once had
wicker cover)
$15.00—20.00

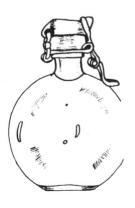

Coffins and Jo Jo Flask
Purple
Basket weave has screw
threads, but ground top
$5.00—8.00

Livingston & Co.
Honey amber, union oval
flask, 7½ in. tall
$100.00+

Flask
Small sunburst punkin
seed; purple, 5 in. tall
$15.00—18.00

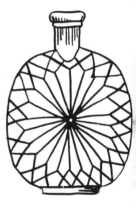

The A. Colburn Co.
Small punkin seed
flask; top is tapered
fluting, below band
are square designs
Purple
$20.00—25.00

S. Grabfelder & Co.
Brown, flat, 6 in. tall
$5.00—6.00

High Grade Liquors
Clear, 1/2 pint flask;
pewter cap, ground top
$5.00—8.00

S. Grabfelder & Co.
Rectangular, purple,
6 in. tall
$5.00—8.00

Dallemand & Co., Inc.
(on two sides and around
base)
Light amber pint flask
$10.00—12.00

Miller's Extra Old
Bourbon
Embossed Trademark
Dark amber, Union oval
flask, 7 1/4 in. tall
$100.00+

Clark's California
Cherry Cordial
Amber, flat, square,
8 1/4 in. tall
$10.00—12.00

Quaker Maid Whiskey (flask)
Fancy embossing around neck
and shoulders
Shades of honey and
dark amber
$10.00—15.00

Vota & Deheines
Clear, pewter cap, ground
top, 7½ in. tall
$5.00—8.00

P. F. Heering
Base inset with 8-pointed
star which is encircled by
''Kiobenhavn''
Red amber, deeply whittle-
marked; also in green;
10½ in. tall
$15.00—25.00

Val Blatz Brewing Co.
Clear with blob top,
7½ in. tall
$6.00—8:00

Thos. McMullen & Co.'s
White Label (etched in glass)
Dark green, 10 in. tall
$4.00—6.00

Johnson Liverpool
Trade Mark Registered —
(on base) S.I.L.B.
Green, 3 pc. mold (ale)
$5.00—7.00

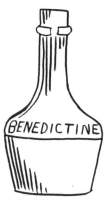

Benedictine
Raised crescent on
opposite side
Dark green, whittle mold
$4.00—6.00

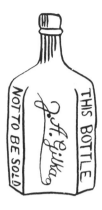

J. A. Gilka – Berlin –
Schutzen Str. – No. 9
Signature on front panel;
embossed figures on
indented base
Amber
$12.00—18.00

E. J. Burke – E.J.B. (on base
around cat with dots
beneath it)
Olive green, bubbly
bottle (stout)
$3.50—4.50

Pabst Brewing Co. –
S.B. & G. Co. (on base)
Brown beer, blob top
$2.00—3.00

Crystal Brewage – Baltimore,
Md.
Carrier pigeon with initials
"C.B." hanging from neck;
thirteen stars & Trademark
Golden color
$75.00+

JSP (interlocking initials)
Initials stand for Jos. S.
Pederson
Blue-green, 9 in. tall,
(malt)
$8.00—10.00

Peter Mugler
Amber, 4-pc. mold, blob
top, 8 in. tall
$3.00—5.00

Cal. Bottling Co. Export
Beer
Brown, blob top, 7 in. tall
$3.00—5.00

Etna Brewing Co. — Etna
Mills, Cal.
Brown, 4-pc. mold, 8 in. tall
$3.00—5.00

John Gillon & Co.'s
King Wm. IV
Dark olive green,
10 in. tall
$10.00—12.00

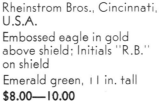

Rheinstrom Bros., Cincinnati,
U.S.A.
Embossed eagle in gold
above shield; Initials "R.B."
on shield
Emerald green, 11 in. tall
$8.00—10.00

Hartwig Kantorowicz
Nachfolger — Berlin
Shape similar to
Gilka
Red amber, 10 1/2
in. tall
$12.00—18.00

Compliments of Hatscher &
Durerr
White crock, 4 in. tall
$4.00—8.00

Ramsay's Superior
Scotch
Malt Whiskey
White crock with
brown handle, 7
in. tall
$15.00—20.00

Compliments of Dupar
McCullough & Plimpton
Tan and brown crock,
3 in. tall
$4.00—6.00

Gde. Chartreuse (etched
in glass)
Clear, 8 in. tall
$6.00—8.00

National Bottling Works
Amber, round
$4.50—5.00

Gilmore's Aromatic Wine
Honey amber, round, 10 in.
tall
$6.00—8.00

Hock Wines
In various shades from teal
blue to ruby red; turn mold,
14 in. tall
$4.00—6.00

Unmarked
Black or olive green,
3-pc. mold, uneven
kick-up base
$8.00—10.00

A. van Hoboken & Co.
Blob seal on shoulder has
initials "AVH."
Dark green, square, case gin
$35.00—40.00

WHISKIES NOT ILLUSTRATED

Americus Club Pure Whiskey (in a circle)
Purple flask, pewter cap, 6 in. tall .... $ 8.00—10.00

Americus Club Pure Whiskey (in a circle)
Amber flask, 6 in. tall .... $ 8.00—10.00

Argonaut E. Martin & Co. — San Francisco, Cal.
(inside a circle) Amber, round .... $15.00—18.00

Crown Distilleries Co. (circling monogram and crown)
Amber, squat, inside threads, 10 in. tall .... $10.00—12.00

J. H. Cutter Old Bourbon — A. P. Hotaling, Sole Agents
Amber, 10 in. tall .... $25.00—30.00

Catto's Whiskey (in script)
Various shades of green, oval, 10¾ in. tall .... $ 8.00—10.00

Chevalier's Old Castle Whiskey — San Francisco, Cal.
Embossed castle, 12 in. tall .... $12.00—15.00

The F. Chevalier Co. Whiskey Merchants (around
interlocking initials) — San Francisco, Cal.
Light amber, 11¾ in. tall .... $20.00—25.00

Cartan-McCarthy and Co. – San Francisco
    Amber, rectangular, 12 in. tall .... **$ 8.00—10.00**

Dallemand & Co. Chicago (around base)
    Amber, fluted shoulders, round, 11 in. tall .... **$ 9.00—12.00**

Donnelly Rye – Full Quart
    Amber, rectangular .... **$ 8.00—10.00**

Jas. Durkin Wine & Liquors – Wholesale & Retail –
Durkin Block – Mill & Sprague – Spokane, Wash.
Telephone Main 731
    Amber, slight bulb neck, 11¾ in. tall .... **$12.00—15.00**

Unmarked
    Four sections in one bottle, each holding a different
    liquor; purple, heavy, 10½ in. tall .... **$25.00—32.00**

Four Roses – Paul Jones Co. – Louisville, Ky. – New
Protective Bottle – Adopted July, 1914
    Leaves and roses embossed in glass .... **$15.00—20.00**

Golden Rule – Braunschweiger & Co. – San Francisco, Cal.
(all in a circle around "XXX Whiskey")
    Amber, round .... **$15.00—18.00**

Hall Luhrs & Co., Sacramento (encircling the interlocking
initials "H.L. Co.")
    Purple, 12 in. tall .... **$12.00—15.00**

Hildebrandt – Posner & Co.
    Aqua, interlocking initials, inside threads; rare! .... **$10.00—25.00**
    Same as above, except amber .... **$10.00—12.00**

Hirsch Malt Whiskey for Medical Use (in circle around
interlocking initials "S.H. Co.")
    Similar in shape to Duffy's Malt .... **$ 6.00— 8.00**

Homer's California Ginger Brandy
    Amber, round .... **$ 6.00— 8.00**

James Woodburn Co., Sacramento, Cal. (circling initials
"J.W. Co.")
    Purple, 12 in. tall .... **$12.00—15.00**

Old Joe Gideon (Bros.) — G. Whiskey — Awarded Gold
Medals at St. Louis, 1904, Portland, Oreg. 1905
    Dark Brown flask ....$ 5.00— 8.00

J. Kellenberger Wholesale Wines & Liquors — Durango,
Colo.
    Clear, round, quart ....$ 8.00—10.00

Monogram Pure Rye Whiskey — Alfred Greenbaum &
Co., Sole Agents
    Brown, squat, 9 in. tall ....$10.00—12.00

Louis Taussig & Co., San Francisco, Cal. (encircling
initials "L.T. Co.")
    Purple, inside threads, 11$\frac{1}{2}$ in. tall ....$10.00—15.00
    Same as above, except amber ....$15.00—18.00

L. T. Co. (Carroll Rye)
    Amber, rectangular ....$ 8.00—10.00

McDonald & Cohn, San Francisco, Cal.
    Purple, rectangular ....$10.00—12.00

Miller's Game Cock Whiskey
    Aqua, 6$\frac{1}{2}$ in. flask ....$ 5.00— 6.50

Mt. Vernon Pure Rye Whiskey
    Amber, square, squat ....$12.00—15.00

Nuyen's (in crude script)
    Dark olive amber, crooked, bulbous neck, 9$\frac{1}{2}$ in. tall ...$18.00—20.00

Old Kaintuck Bourbon
    Rectangular, 4 in. tall (miniature) ....$ 8.00—10.00

Oregon Importing Co., Portland, Ore. (encircling "We
Neither Rectify Nor Compound")
    Amber, fluted shoulders ....$20.00—25.00

The Old Bushmill Distillery Co., Limited — Est. 1784 —
still (embossed) — Trade Mark
    Aqua, square ....$ 8.00—12.00

Paul Jones Pure Rye — Louisville, Ky. (on blob seal on shoulder)
    Brown, squat .... $ 6.00— 8.00

Picnic flasks
    Punkin seed flasks, purple, small to large .... $ 5.00— 6.00

Kreiel Sheimer Bros., Seattle, Wash. (below a diamond with interlocking initials) — Crown Diamonds (on reverse)
    Light amber, 11 in. tall .... $12.00—15.00

Red Top Rye (embossed spinning top) — Westheimer & Sons — Louisville, Ky.
    Red amber .... $ 8.00—10.00

Siebe Bros. & Plageman — San Francisco
    Inside threads, rectangular .... $ 8.00—12.00

Unmarked
    Shaped like miniature punkin seed; embossed star in center, oval flask; about 2 oz.; 3½ in. tall .... $ 8.00—10.00

Slater's Premium Bourbon — John Sroufe & Co., Sole Agents, San Francisco
    Amber .... $ 8.00—10.00

Taylor & Williams, Louisville, Ky.
    Purple, round .... $ 5.00— 8.00

Dr. Warren's Pure Ginger Brandy — Homer Williams & Co., Proprietors, San Francisco
    Amber .... $ 5.00— 6.00

W. J. Van Schuyver & Co., Inc. — Portland, Ore.
    Embossed crown above initial "V" which is inside a square; Amber, inside threads .... $12.00—15.00

J. Aronson Full Measure, Seattle, Wash.
    Amber, round. 12 in. tall .... $ 9.00—12.00

Sunset Wine House, 1919 Hewitt St. — Everett, Wash. (heavily embossed in a circle)
    Honey amber, bulbous neck, 11 in. tall .... $12.00—15.00

The Shawhan Distillery Co. (around base)
    Purple; fluting around neck & shoulders; 12 in. tall ....**$ 8.00—10.00**

Williams Yesler Way & Occidental — Seattle, Wash.
(embossed in circle)
    Purple, 1/4 pnt. punkin seed ....**$15.00—18.00**

Weil Bros. & Sons — San Francisco
    Purple, square/also in amber and round ....**$10.00—12.00**

Wright & Taylor Distillers — Louisville, Ky. — Registered
    Brown, squat ....**$ 8.00—10.00**

U.S. Mail Box Rye — U.S. Mail (on side panels)
Paper label reads: Rheinstrom Bros., Sole Agents
    Eagle on side panels ....**$25.00—30.00**

Our Choice Old Bourbon — Hencken & Schroeder —
208–210 Front St., S. F. — Sole Agents
    Amber ....**$25.00—30.00**

Unmarked Whiskey
    Yellow-green, whittle mold, long neck, 12 in. tall ....**$ 8.00—10.00**

N. M. Uri & Co., Louisville, Ky.
    Amber flask, fluting around shoulders & sides, 6 1/2
    in. tall ....**$12.00—15.00**

Crown Distilleries Company (around "Trade Mark,"
crown and shield)
    Honey amber, inside threads, 6 in. tall ....**$18.00—20.00**

Amer. Picon — Phillipeville
    Green; embossed hand, bulbous neck, 3-pc. mold, 12
    in. tall ....**$10.00—12.00**

Asparagus Gin — The Rothenberg Co.
    Light green, round, 10 1/2 in. tall ....**$ 8.00—10.00**

Hudson's Bay Co., Incorporated 1670
    Purple, round, 11 3/4 in. tall ....**$?**

BEER, ALES, WINES, ETC., NOT ILLUSTRATED

Arnas (on base)
  Light amber, whittle mold, 8 in. tall .... $ 2.50— 4.00

Barner & Reiber Bottlers — Redding, Cal.
  Amber, 4-pc. mold, 11½ in. tall .... $ 3.00— 5.00

Buffalo Brewing Co., Sacramento, Cal. (encircling a
buffalo and horseshoe in raised relief)
  Amber .... $ 6.00— 8.00

Florida Wine Co., Philada., Pa., U.S.A.
  Purple, round, laid-on ring, 11¾ in. tall .... $ 6.00— 9.00

Garrett & Co. — Established in 1835 — American
Wines — St. Louis, Mo.
  Purple, 12 in. tall .... $ 3.00— 4.00

Garrett & Co. — Established 1835 — St. Louis, Mo. —
Norfolk, Va. — American Wines (around embossed
eagle on shield)
  Purple, 6 in. tall (miniature) .... $ 5.00— 6.00

Hoefer & Mevius Bottlers — Redding, Cal.
  Amber .... $ 3.00— 5.00

Fink & Mugler Bottlers — Keswick, Cal.
  Light amber, 8 in. tall .... $ 3.00— 5.00

AVH (on blob seal on shoulder)
  Dark olive green, square, case Gin .... $25.00—35.00
  Same as above with initials on blob seal, no embossing .. $20.00—25.00
  Similar, but no writing; whittled .... $ 8.00—10.00

Johann Hoff (around shoulders)
  Dark green, squat, 7½ in. tall .... $ 5.00— 6.00

Kahny & Burgbacher Bottlers — Redding, Cal. (vertically)
  Amber, 4-pc. mold, 8 in. tall .... $ 3.00— 5.00

Meamber Bros. Bottlers — Yreka, Cal.
  Amber, 11 in. tall .... $ 3.00— 4.00

Merrasoul Bros., San Francisco (all within a circle)
  Amber, 4-pc. mold, 8 in. tall ....$ 3.00— 5.00

National Lager Beer — H. Rohrbacher, Agent,
Stockton, Cal.
  Amber, 11 in. tall ....$ 3.00— 5.00

Original Big 6 Gin
  Purple, rectangular ....$ 8.00—10.00

Mt. Shasta Bottling Works — Mugler Bros. — Sisson, Cal.
  Amber, 11 in. tall ....$ 5.00— 6.00

J. Personeni New York (circling crown Trade Mark
and "J. P.")
  Aqua, slight bulbous neck, 11 in. tall ....$ 4.00— 6.00

Schuster's Malt Extract (around shoulders)
  Brown, squat crown cap ....$ 2.50— 3.00

John Wieland's Extra Pale — Cal. Bottling Co. (on
reverse, etched)
  Aqua, round, 9½ in. tall ....$ 8.00—10.00

Rainier Beer, Seattle Brewing & Malting Co.
  Dark amber, 7¾ in. tall ....$ 5.00— 7.00

WESTWARD THE BOTTLE

After the Revolutionary War, when distilleries and breweries had become quite common, the clipper ships of the day conveyed liquor flasks around the Horn to quench the thirst of the miners in the gold fields. Liquor made life endurable to those subjected to loneliness, the elements, and a diet of beans and sow belly for weeks on end.

Never did a wagon train leave the east without a good supply of some type of liquor aboard. The comforts of the trail were few, and around the campfire at night, after a trying day of dust, sweat, and toil, a shot of "red eye" would help soothe raw nerves.

If one had scruples about taking whiskey, he could still retain his respectability with a bottle of Hostetter's Bitters or Paine's Celery Compound. Unfortunately, some of this "firewater" or "Taos Lightning" taken as a medicine for fever, chills, or malaria acquired the reputation of either killing or curing, depending on the ruggedness of the individual.

The whiskey salesman traveling about the West passed out miniature bottles of liquor as samples to drum up business. Some of these had labels; those with the greatest value to today's collector were embossed with the trade name, bottler, or distiller. In all the ghost towns in which we dig, we invariably come up with some of these highly prized miniatures. Nothing better represents the joys and ills of the everyday lives of the early pioneers than the old bottles that collectors are uncovering today.

BITTERS

St. Drake's Plantation X
Bitters — 1860 Patented
(on roof)
From dark to honey amber,
square, 10 in. tall
$22.00—28.00

Boker's Stomach Bitters
(label)
Golden amber (as well as
various other shades); long,
bulbous neck — called lady's
leg; 11 in. tall
$30.00—50.00

P. L. Abbey Co.,
Kalamazoo, Mich. (on
base)
Kalamazoo Celery Pepsin
Bitters (label)
Clear, square, lady's
leg neck, 8 in. tall
$12.00—18.00

Pepsin Calisaya Bitters
Dr. Russell Med.
Co. (on side)
Green, flat
$18.00—25.00

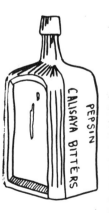

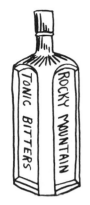

Rocky Mountain – Tonic
Bitters – 1840 Try Me
1870 (each on one of three
panels)
Golden amber; rare!
(6-star, Watsons)
$75.00—85.00

Peruvian Bitters
Fancy monogram on reverse
side
Clear or amber, square
$18.00—22.00

(Bourbon)
Roehling & Schutz, Inc.,
Chicago (near base) –
R.S. Co. (near eaves)
Shaped similarly to
Doyle's Hop Bitters
Six rows of shakes on
roof
$30.00—40.00

Yerba Buena Bitters, S.F.
Cal. (down sides of coffin-
shaped flask)
Dark to golden amber
$50.00—??

Amaro di Felsino G. Buton
& G (around shoulders)
Tonic Bitters (since 1874)
Beautiful olive green, lady's
leg neck, 15 in. tall
$55.00—70.00

Ernst L. Arp Kiel
Older ones have blob seal
on shoulder
Aqua, 13 to 15 in. tall
$25.00—??

Doyle's Hop Bitters —
1872 (on shoulder)
Hops hanging from leaf on
front panel
Dark amber, square
$22.00—28.00

Dr. Harter's Wild Cherry
Bitters
Amber, wide, flat
$18.00—22.00

Dr. L. E. Keeley's Double
Chloride of Gold Cure for
Drunkenness
K.G.C. Leslie E. Keeley,
M.D. (in script on curved
back)
Clear, 6 in. tall
$25.00—30.00

BITTERS NOT ILLUSTRATED

Abbott's Aromatic Bitters (on metal cap) — C. W.
Abbott & Co., Baltimore (around shoulders and on base)
   Brown, 8 in. tall .... $ 4.00— 6.00

Atwood's Jaundice Bitters — Formerly Made by Moses
Atwood, Georgetown, Mass.
   Aqua, 12-sided, 6 in. tall .... $ 4.00— 5.00

Brown's Iron Bitters — Brown Chemical Co.
  Brown, square, 8½ in. tall ....$18.00—20.00

California Fig Bitters (on front panel) — California
Extract of Fig Co., San Francisco, Cal. (on back panel)
  Light amber, square, 9¾ in. tall ....$35.00—45.00

Caroni Bitters (around shoulders and on base)
  Dark green, 8½ in. tall ....$ 6.00—10.00

Celebrated Crown Bitters (on front panel) — F. Chevalier
& Co., Sole Agents (on back panel)
  Light amber, square, 9 in. tall ....$65.00—75.00

Dunkley Celery Co., Kalamazoo, Mich. (on base)
Celery Pepsin Bitters
  Clear, square, 6½ in. tall ....$12.00—18.00

Electric Bitters (on front panel) — H. E. Bucklin & Co.,
Chicago, Ill. (on back panel)
  Brown, square ....$20.00—22.00

Ferro—Quina Stomach Bitters Blood Maker —
Manufactured by D. P. Rossi — San Francisco, Cal.
  Amber, square, squat, short bulb neck ....$35.00—40.00

Ferro China Bisleri (around shoulders) — Milano (near base)
  Olive green, round, whittle mold ....$10.00—12.00

Fratella Branca—Milano (on blob seal on shoulder)
  Green, turn mold, 10 in. tall ....$ 5.00— 6.00

H.A.U. (interlocking on base)
  Red amber, round, heavy, lady's leg neck (Underberg)....$10.00—15.00

Dr. Hostetter's Stomach Bitters
  Amber, square, various initials on base ....$ 6.00—10.00

Hoofland's German Bitters (on front panel) — C. M. Jackson,
Philadelphia (on back panel) — Dyspepsia & C Liver
Complaint (on side panels)
  Aqua, rectangular, 7¾ in. tall ....$25.00—35.00

Lash's Kidney & Liver Bitters — The Best Cathartic &
Blood Purifier
    Amber, square .... $ 5.00— 7.00

Marshall's Bitters — The Best Laxative & Blood Purifier
    Brown, square .... $20.00—30.00

Reed's Bitters
    Same shape as Boker's .... $30.00—45.00

Rex Kidney & Liver Bitters
    Amber, square .... $15.00—18.00

Dr. J. G. B. Siegert's & Hijos (around shoulders; on base)
    Olive green, round .... $ 5.00— 8.00

Dr. Walker's V.B. (on base)
    Aqua, round .... $12.00—15.00

Toneco Stomach Bitters (on front) — Appetizer & Tonic
(on back)
    Clear, square (5-star, rare!) .... $45.00—50.00

CURE-ALLS FOR MAN AND BEAST

During the last half of the nineteenth century, the medicine man or drummer traveled through the West selling his concoctions to eager customers, often hawking them from the back of a wagon. Taken internally or externally, his patent medicines were reputed to soothe and cure every ailment of man and beast at the price of $1.00 per bottle.

The old ghost towns, early mining camps, and homesteads have yielded interesting finds in these old medicine bottles. One cobalt blue bottle has the following label: "Sanford's Radical Cure for Catarrh: Instantly relieves and permanently cures acute, chronic and ulcerative catarrh, plus nervous headache, neuralgia, earache, ringing noises in the head, deafness, ulcerated sore throat, bleeding of the lungs, sore and weak eyes, etc." All for the price of $1.00!

Another, "Fenner's Peoples Remedy—Kidney and Back-ache—1872–1898" was used with the hope of dissolving kidney stones and curing catarrh of the bladder. A pretty, pale aqua bottle, labeled "Osgood's India Chologogue," held a purgative which allegedly stimulated the functioning of the liver. A ten-sided aqua miniature contained "Kendall's Spavin Cure," used simply for "Human Flesh." And frostbite, swellings, and wounds on man and beast were often treated with "Gargling Oil."

Dr. D. Jayne's Medical Almanac contains this doctor's testimonial for 1850: "I have prescribed Dr. Jayne's Tonic Vermifuge in many cases of worms and fever caused by worms. I recommend it to all who have children. If adults would use it, we would not see so many haggard faces in our land."

"Dr. Thompson's Eye Water" was very popular, too. A volume dated 1884 furnished the article on eye water from which the following excerpt is taken: "If this causes too much smarting in bad cases, reduce some of it with more rain water, so that it shall not smart more then five minutes at most."

The same volume had this recipe for red sealing wax for bottling medicine: Rosin, 1 1/4 lbs.; tallow, lard, and beeswax, each 1 oz. Melt together and add American Vermilion, 1 oz. Dip while hot. Druggists dipped their vial corks in the wax or resealed bottles after the cork had been cut off. Today, bottles are often found with this sealing wax still discernible around the lip.

POISON BOTTLES

It was not until the 1830s that any attempt was made to safeguard purchasers of poisonous substances by requiring a label on the bottle that called attention to the dangers of the ingredients. And not until 1858 were any bottles made with the word **poison** embossed in the glass.

Then, in 1872, what would become the most widely used poison bottle, manufactured by Whitall, Tatum, and Co., was put into production. However, most of the bottles being found today are a product of "H.B. and Co." (which is stamped on the base), and date from around World War I. They were made from a deep, cobalt blue glass and molded in sizes ranging to sixteen ounces. The surface of the bottles was marked with a diamond-shaped design, while the stopper surface was covered with sharp points in such a manner that it would be impossible to remove the stopper without the fingers coming in contact with the points.

Three of the most interesting poison bottles are pictured below, among the first to employ the skull and crossbones motif which has signified danger and death for centuries. In 1890, the coffin-shaped bottle entered into production. 1893 saw the advent of the bone-

shaped poison bottle. Probably the most intriguing of them all, though, is the skull-shaped bottle patented in 1894. It is impossible to say how many of these bottles were manufactured, yet the field of poison bottles is proving to be a rich and exciting one.

MEDICINES AND CURES

Poison (on glass)
Sharp-pointed stopper;
bottle has diamond
quilted pattern; cobalt,
4 sizes: 4½, 5½,
6½, and 8 in. tall
$8.00—12.00
set—**$35.00**

Owl Drug Co.
Blue-green, also in emerald
green; 10 in. tall
$15.00—18.00

The Owl Drug Co.
Cobalt, 3-sided; 3½, 4, 6
in. tall
$8.00—15.00

Gargling Oil, Lockport, N.Y.
Lockport green, also lighter
green; 6 in. tall
$8.00—10.00

Osgood's India
Chologogue, New York
Aqua, very short neck
$3.00—5.00

Kendall's Spavin Cure for
Human Flesh – Enosburgh
Falls, Vt.
Aqua, 10-sided, 5¼ in. tall
$3.00—4.00

Dr. Peter's Blood
Vitalizer –
B.P. 1780–1880 Trade
Mark (on back panel
with slim tree in
raised relief)
Purple, oblong
$2.00—2.50

Dr. Wistar's Balsam of Wild
Cherry – Philada.
Aqua, 8-sided, 7 and 5 in.
tall
$6.00—8.00

Ayer's Hair Vigor
(color restorer)
Beautiful peacock blue,
also in cobalt; 6½
in. tall
$25.00—35.00

Dr. E. Champlain – Ligneous
Extract
Blue–green; bubbly whittle
mold, 5¾ in. tall
$6.00—8.00

Buckingham Whisker Dye
(on side panels)
Brown, 5 in. tall
$5.00—6.00

R. C. & A. New York
(around shoulders)
Cobalt, round, 9 in. tall
$3.00—6.00

Kelly's Rheumatic Syrup
Aqua, 5½ in. tall
$3.00—4.00

Dr. Thompson's Eye Water –
New London, Connt.
Aqua, round, 4 in. tall
$1.50—2.00

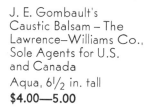

J. E. Gombault's
Caustic Balsam – The
Lawrence–Williams Co.,
Sole Agents for U.S.
and Canada
Aqua, 6½ in. tall
$4.00—5.00

Botanic Cough Balsam (on
front panel) – Dr. Warren's;
S.F. Cal. (on side panels)
Aqua, 8 in. tall
$4.00—5.00

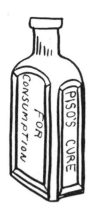

Piso's Cure for Consumption — Hazeltine & Co.
Pale green and emerald green
$1.50—2.50

Dr. Pierce's Propr. (on side panel) — Catarrh Remedy (on back panel) — Dr. Sage's, Buffalo (on side panels)
Approx. 2 in. tall
$2.00—3.00

Humphrey's Homeopathic
Horse's head in raised relief; clear, 3 in. tall
$3.50—4.00

The Empire Nursing Bottle
Interlocking initials in center of bottle are "W.T. Co."
Clear, curved neck
$10.00—12.00

The Graduated Nursing Bottle — (ounce no. on opposite side)
Purple, oval
$8.00—10.00

Carlo Erba Milano (on front panel) — Olio—Ricino (on reverse)
Clear, 5 in. tall
$1.00—1.50

Prescribed by R. V.
Pierce, M.D.
7 in. tall
$3.00—4.00

Dr. Henley's Celery, Beef,
and Iron – C.B. & I Extract
Co., S.F., Cal.
Brown, 9 in. tall
$4.00—6.00

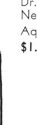

Dr. Miles Restorative
Nervine
Aqua, 7½ in. tall
$1.00—1.25

The Clinic Blood Purifier
Aqua, 9½ in. tall
$3.00—5.00

A Texas Wonder
Aqua
$2.00—3.00

Bro. Benjamin's Herbalo
Blood Purifier – Stomach,
Liver and Kidney Renovator
Pale green, 8½ in. tall
$4.00—6.00

Warner's Safe Kidney &
Liver Cure
Picture of safe in
raised relief
Brown, 9 in. tall
$9.00—10.00

Dr. M. M. Fenner's Peoples
Remedy
Brown, rectangular, 10½
in. tall
$10.00—12.00

H.H.H. Horse Medicine
D.D.T. 1868
Aqua, 6 in. tall
$2.50—4.00

Ess—Tee—Dee Success
Destroys Dandruff
Barber bottle
$4.00—6.00

Enfield Reynold's Gout
Specific
Clear, square, heavy glass,
3½ in. tall
$2.00—3.00

John Wyeth & Brother
(vertically) – Take Next Dose
At (around base of neck—
cap gives prescribed time)
Cobalt, square
$5.00—6.00

Shiloh's Consumption Cure
S. C. Wells, Leroy, N.Y.
Aqua, 6½ in. tall
$2.50—4.00

Owl Drug (emblem for
Standard Pharmaceuticals)
Square, rounded corners
$2.00—4.00

Dr. Kilmer's Swamp Root
Aqua, 7¼ in. tall
$3.00—4.00

Hall's Balsam for the Lungs
(on front panel) — Foley &
Co., Chicago, U.S.A.
(on side panels)
Aqua, 8½ in. tall
$4.50—5.00

The Great Dr. Kilmer's
Swamp Root
Aqua, 8¼ in. tall
$2.50—3.00

Foley's Kidney & Bladder
Cure (on front panel)—Foley
& Co., Chicago U.S.A.
(on side panels)
Brown, rectangular, 9 in. tall
$6.00—8.00

Gun Wa's Chinese Remedy —
Warranted Entirely
Vegetable & Harmless
Golden with greenish tinge,
square; rare!
$15.00—18.00

Wakefield's Cough Syrup
Aqua
$2.50—3.00

Dr. Price's Florida Water
Purple
$4.00—5.00

Solon Palmer's Florida Water
Aqua, 6½ in. tall
$4.00—5.00

Old Colonial Bay Rum
The S. H. Wetmore Co.
Amber, 7½ in. tall
$3.50—4.00

MEDICINES AND CURES NOT ILLUSTRATED

Ayer's (on front panel) – Cherry Pectoral (on sides) – Lowell,
Mass. (on back)
Aqua, 7½ in. tall .... $ 3.00— 4.00

Ayer's Sarsaparilla – Lowell, Mass. U.S.A.
Aqua .... $ 5.00— 6.00

Barry's Tricopherous for the Skin & Hair
Aqua .... $ 3.00— 4.00

Bachelor's Superior Hair Dye No. 1
Aqua, square, scarred base, 3 in. tall .... $ 4.00— 6.00

Dr. Boschee's German Syrup – L. M. Green, Proprietor
Aqua, rectangular, 7 in. tall .... $ 3.00— 4.00

B. A. Fahnstock's Vermifuge
Aqua, round, 4 in. tall .... $ 1.00— 1.50

Burnett's Cocaine (on front panel) Burnett – Boston (on
side panels
Aqua, 7 in. tall .... $ 4.00— 5.00

Dr. O. Phelps Brown (on front panel)
Aqua, rectangular, 8 in. tall .... $ 3.50— 4.00

Dr. Burney's Catarrhal Powder
Clear, sheared lip, round, 3 in. tall .... $ 2.00— 4.00

Citrate of Magnesia
Purple, wire and porcelain stopper .... $ 1.50— 2.00

Doct. Marshall's Catarrh Snuff
Aqua, square, heavy, 3½ in. tall .... $ 2.50— 3.00

Dr. McMunn's Elixir of Opium
Aqua, round, 4½ in. tall .... $ 3.00— 5.00

Chamberlain's Colic, Cholera & Diarrhea Remedy
Aqua, rectangular, 4½ in. tall .... $ 1.50— 2.00

Chamberlain's Pain Balm
Aqua, rectangular .... $ 1.50— 2.00

Chamberlain's Cure for Consumption
Aqua, rectangular .... $ 2.00— 3.00

Chesebrough Mfg. Co. Vaseline
Purple, also amber; wide mouth, 3 in. tall .... $ .25— .50

Dickey Chemist, S. F. – Pioneer 1850
Brown, also cobalt; design of mortar and pestle;
rectangular .... $ 4.00— 6.00

Ely's Cream Balm, New York – Catarrh & Hay Fever
(on sides)
Brown, 2½ in. tall .... $ 1.50— 2.00

Floraplexion – Cures Dyspepsia, Liver Complaint &
Consumption (in sunken front panel); Franklin – Hart
(in side panels)
Aqua, rectangular, 6½ in. tall .... $ 3.00— 4.00

For the Hair (on front panel) – Lyons (on back) – Kathairon
& New York (on sides) .... $ 2.50— 3.00

Frederick Stearns & Co., Detroit, Mich. (down
bevelled corner)
Brown, triangular, 10 in. tall .... $ 2.50— 3.00

B. P. Co. (on front, with initials PP back to back
within circle)
Cobalt, oval, 3 in. tall (Camphor?) .... $ 8.00—10.00

Glover's Imperial Distemper Cure – H. Clay Glover,
New York
Brown, rectangular .... $ .50— .75

Dr. Gunn's Onion Syrup
Aqua, sample size .... $ 1.50— 2.00

Dr. Harter's Soothing Drops
Aqua, round, 5 in. tall .... $ 2.00— 2.50

Hall's Catarrh Cure
Aqua, round, 4½ in. tall .... $ 2.00— 3.00

Herbine (a compound of herbs used in the treatment
of temporary constipation) .... $ 1.00— 1.50

Dr. D. Jayne's Expectorant (for cough)
Aqua, rectangular .... $ 3.00— 4.00

Dr. D. Jayne's Tonic Vermifuge Strength Giver
Aqua, rectangular .... $ 3.00— 4.00

W. H. Hooker & Co. Sole Agents North and South
America — Acker's Blood Elixir & for all Blood Diseases
Brown, rectangular, 7 in. tall .... $ 3.00— 4.00

Hay's Hair Health (on side panels)
Brown, rectangular, 6¾ in. tall .... $ 2.00— 3.00

Hoff's Liniment — Goodrich Drug Co. — Anoka, Minn.
Aqua, 12-sided .... $ 2.00— 2.50

Kemp's Balsam for Throat & Lungs (on front panel) — O.
F. Woodward, Leroy, New York (on side panels)
Aqua .... $ 4.00— 5.00

Kendall's Spavin Cure (around shoulders)
Brown, 10-sided .... $ 2.00— 3.00

Dr. King's New Cure for Consumption
Aqua, rectangular .... $ 2.00— 2.50

Dr. King's New Life Pills — H. E. Bucklin & Co., Chicago,
U.S.A.
2½ in. tall .... $ 1.00— 1.50

Kennedy's Medical Discovery (on side panel) — Roxbury,
Mass., U.S.A. (on front panel)
Aqua, rectangular .... $ 4.00— 5.00

Laxol — A. J. White — New York (all vertically in two
front panels)
Cobalt, rounded back panel; 7 in. tall .... $ 6.00— 8.00

Minard's Liniment
Aqua .... $ 1.50— 2.00

Lydia Pinkham's Vegetable Compound
   Purple .... $ 2.00— 2.50

Mexican Mustang Liniment — Lyon Mfg. Co., New York
   Purple, also aqua; round .... $ 3.00— 3.50

The Mother's Friend — Bradfield Reg'l Co. — Atlanta, Ga.
   Green, 7 in. tall .... $ 2.00— 3.00

Paine's Celery Compound (in two panels)
   Amber, square, 10 in. tall .... $ 3.00— 4.00

Pepto Mangan Gude
   Aqua, 6-sided .... $ 1.50— 2.00

Dr. Pierce's Golden Medical Discovery
   Aqua, rectangular, 9 in. tall .... $ 1.50— 2.00

R. V. Pierce, M.D. (on side panel) — Extract of Smart
Weed; Buffalo, N.Y. (on front panel) — Dr. Pierce (in
curved back panel) T. W. Co. (on base)
   Aqua, rectangular, 6 in. tall .... $ 6.00— 8.00

Pioneer 1850 (with design of mortar and pestle)
   Light cobalt, rectangular (older Dickey Chemist?) .... $ 8.00—10.00

R. R. R. Radway & Co., New York (on front panel) —
Ent'd. Accord. to Act of Congress [Cure for pain,
"Radway's Ready Relief"]
   Aqua, rectangular, 7½ in. tall .... $ 3.00— 4.00

Rumford's Chemical Works (vertically in two slim
panels—initial "W" above)
   Blue-green, 8-sided .... $10.00—12.00

Sanford's Radical Cure (on side panels) — Potter
Drug & Chemical Corporation, Boston, Mass., U.S.A.
(on base) [Paper label: "Cure for Catarrh, etc."]
   Cobalt, 7½ in. tall .... $ 6.00— 8.00

Save—The—Horse — Registered Trade Mark —
Treatment for Lameness — Troy Chemical Co.,
Binghamton, N.Y. (all in sunken panel)
   Pale green, 6½ in. tall .... $ 3.00— 4.00

Silver Pine Healing Oil
Aqua, rectangular, 8 in. tall .... $ 1.00— 1.50

Schenck's Pulmonic Syrup — Philada.
Aqua, 8-sided .... $ 5.00— 6.00

Sloan's Anti Colic
Clear, square, 5 in. tall .... $ 2.00— 2.50

Sozodont (on two side panels) — For the Teeth and
Breath (on front panel)
Purple, 2 in. tall .... $ 1.50— 2.00

St. Jacob's Oel — The Charles A. Vogeler Company —
Baltimore, Md., U.S.A.
Aqua, round, 6½ in. tall .... $ 2.00— 3.00

Smith's Bile Beans (in a circle, half dollar size)
Clear, 2 in. tall .... $ 3.50— 4.00

Dr. Sage's — Buffalo (on side panels) — Catarrh remedy
(on front panel) .... $ 2.00— 3.00

A. Trask's Magnetic Ointment
Aqua, square, 3½ in. tall .... $ 1.50— 2.00

Twiaba — Warranted (on side panels)
Blue-green, 7 in. tall .... $ 2.00— 2.50

Watkin's Liniment for Man & Beast
Aqua, rectangular .... $ 1.00— 1.50

Mrs. Winslow's Soothing Syrup — Curtis & Perkins,
Proprietors
Aqua, round, 5 in. tall .... $ 2.00— 3.00

Dr. Winchell's Teething Syrup — Emmert Proprietory
Co., Chicago, Ill.
Purple, round, 5 in. tall .... $ 2.50— 3.00

Downing's Soothing Anodyne — Madison Medicine Co.
Sole Proprietors of Downing's Family Medicines;
Madison, Wis. — For Colic, Nervous Tremors,
Twitchings, Hysterics, etc.
   Aqua, round, 4½ in. tall ....$ 2.00— 3.00

The Duffy Malt Whiskey Co. — Rochester, N.Y., U.S.A.
(in circle around initials "D.M.W. Co.")
   Brown, round, 10 in. tall ....$ 4.00— 6.00

ALONG FRONTIER TRAILS

On returning from our first bottle hunting trip, we found that we had also collected an assortment of junk: old ox shoes, buttons, early day marbles, and many other discarded relics of bygone days. Tossed in a heap in a corner of our shed, they remained unnoticed until a few years ago. Today, however, these artifacts of Western Americana are collectors' items and are among some of our most prized finds.

Discovering our first sun-colored purple insulator sent us on a search for other varieties and colors, many of which have since been found along the trails to the ghost towns of the West. The ultimate in a collection of this kind, of course, is the wooden and metal insulator from the transcontinental telegraph line that was constructed in 1861 and paralleled the Pony Express route from St. Joseph, Missouri, to Sacramento, California.

In the summer of 1966, we prowled the ruins of old Ft. Stambaugh, Wyoming. It had been constructed in 1861 to safeguard the miners in the area as well as protect the emigrant trains traveling across the South Pass from marauding Indians. Our party turned up several shell casings, mule shoes, a soldier's cavalry button, and an ivory poker chip. Small finds that they were, they well reflect the nature of life at this old army post.

On our way home we stopped off at the ghost town of Hamilton, Nevada, and began a search in earnest for the elusive bottles. The town had already been hunted thoroughly by others since our first visit there several years before, so we headed for the outskirts to use our potato rakes and shovels in the sagebrush. After some time we were rewarded with a large crock ale, several small embossed medicines, an older Gargling Oil, some delicate aqua umbrella inks and some embossed barrel mustards, both of which have open pontils. But one of the rare finds was a light cobalt, long-necked bottle with "Pioneer 1850" and a mortar and pestle embossed on one side, believed to be the older Dickey Chemist bottle.

Along with some nice bottles, eleven year old Johnnie Nelson found an 1873 C. C. mint quarter in very good condition. It wasn't until he arrived home that he discovered the coin to be valued at over $325.00!

We also visited the ghost town of Treasure City, high on windswept Treasure Peak above Hamilton. This once rich town was built on the side of an extremely rocky hill where we found shards of many beautiful bottles that had failed to survive the terrain and the elements. Among the hundreds of broken pieces, once in a while a whole bottle was unearthed: one small cone-shaped crock ink, a Pioneer Soda, and several small Bachelor's Hair Dyes with open pontils. The biggest thrill of all came when Johnnie's mother dug a "lady's leg" bitters. Our finds were a blue-green J. Walker's V. B. (vinegar bitters) and a tall, yellow-green whiskey, different from any we have.

A beginning collector should not be discouraged when a site appears thoroughly culled of its bottles. A systematic and careful search on the outskirts will usually reward him; sagebrush and a small amount of soil often conceal a choice bottle or relic. Persistence, patience, and hard work are the tools of the bottle hunter, as the following incident will illustrate.

After leaving Hamilton, Roy and Elvine Geinger of Chilonquin, Oregon, decided to scout the area several miles south of Eureka, Nevada. They had promised to notify us when they located a good prospect. The first evening, near their encampment, they found a Paul Jones whiskey in the sagebrush. Early the next morning they began sinking test holes in an area that had been scoured previously by hundreds of bottle hunters. Within a short time Roy, with pick and shovel, broke through the clay into rust seams and broken glass at a depth of about six feet. Every so often he would uncover a fine embossed whiskey, occasionally with inside threads. When we arrived, five of us began sinking holes. In the meantime, Roy unearthed Roths with inside threads, an old Castle, a C. H. Moore, a Green's Lung Restorer, a Dr. Pierce's Extract of Smart Weed, and many more. Every bottle that was removed Elvine wrapped in newspaper to prevent cracking due to temperature changes. Although our test holes proved barren, Roy had struck a partially filled mine shaft and a jackpot of bottles.

Within all of us a little of the pioneer spirit's wanderlust remains, urging us to probe the old ghost towns and abandoned homesteads, to tramp the hills and canyons in search of solitude and treasure. What cheers us is that there are countless sites left to hunt and innumerable bottles that still wait to be found.

MINERAL WATERS AND SODAS

In various places throughout the West, especially in California, there are natural soda springs where water comes out of the earth thirty percent carbonated. Between 1850 and the turn of the century, a number of firms were employed in the process of bottling this natural mineral water for distribution to the surrounding towns and states. Many companies brought their name bottles to one spring for filling. These beautiful bottles, often similar in shape but varying in color from shades of aqua, ice-blue, light and deep cobalt to pale and deep greens, are much sought after by the collector.

The "pops" are more valuable today, not because of their color but because of the oddity of their shapes. Some, for instance, have beveled bases; others, eight or ten sides.

There were also the mineral springs whose bottled contents did not provide a pop when opened. This water was bottled in larger containers similar to the old slope-shouldered beers. Each had its name in the glass, such as Allen or Fouts or Bartlett.

Incidentally, any soda bottle bearing the name "Sac City" is over 100 years old.

Tolenas Soda Springs —
Natural Mineral Water
Aqua, blob lip, 7 in.
tall
$6.00—8.00

McEwin — San Francisco
10-sided
Aqua, blob lip
$8.00—10.00

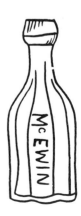

Jackson's Napa Soda
Spring's — Natural Mineral
Water
Aqua, blob lip, 7½ in.
tall
$6.00—7.00

Ross's Belfast (ginger ale)
Round bottom
$4.00—6.00

Seltsers—Nassau (near base)
Tall pottery with handle
$6.00—8.00

Lytton Geyser Soda
Springs — Natural Mineral
Water
Dark blue-green; 4-pc. mold
$8.00—10.00

Unmarked
Plain green; round
with wire stopper
$4.00—5.00

American Soda Works — S. F.
Flag has thirteen stars;
Blob top; also old crown cap
$6.00—8.00

MINERAL WATERS AND SODAS NOT ILLUSTRATED

Allen Mineral Water (vertically)
   Amber, slope shoulder .... $ 3.00— 4.00

Baldwin Tuthill & Co. – 112 Warren St. – N.Y.
   Green, blob top .... $ 8.00—10.00

Bernardino Natural Springs Water (encircling) The A.
Goux Co. – P.C.G.W. (on base)
   Aqua, 5 gal. demijohn .... $20.00—25.00

Abilena (on base)
   Red Amber, blob top, also collared lip, 6 in. tall .... $ 3.00— 4.00

Bartell Springs Mineral Water – California–Anderson
Bottlg. Co., S.F. (etched on reverse)
   Aqua, whittle mold, 9½ in. tall .... $ 8.00—10.00

Bay City Soda Water Co., S.F.
   Blue, 5-pointed star (on reverse) .... $20.00—25.00

Carlsbad (on base)
   Olive green, whittle mold .... $ 8.00—10.00

Camer & Jacky – Phillipsburg, Mont.
   Aqua, blob top, 6¾ in. tall .... $ 6.00— 7.00

Cantrell & Cochran – Belfast & Dublin
   Round bottomed ginger ale .... $4.00— 6.00

J. A. Dearborn – New York – Mineral Water
   Deep blue-green, star (on shoulder), 8-sided .... $12.00—15.00

Dyottville Glass Works (in an arch) – Philada.
   Aqua, blob top .... $ 8.00—12.00

G.L.M. – Prescott, Ariz.
   Aqua, 4-pc. mold, old crown cap .... $ 2.00— 3.00

Henry Burrhard, 18th & Jefferson St., Chicago – H.B.
(on base)
   Aqua .... $ 6.00— 8.00

Holden's G. A. Capitol Soda Works – Sac. (on base)
Ice blue, whittle mold, beveled base, 9 in. tall ....$18.00—20.00

H – Sac. – P (on reverse)
Ice blue, blob top .... $12.00—15.00

Jackson's Napa Soda, S.F.
Amber, slope shoulder, 9½ in. tall ....$ 3.00— 4.00

Lancaster X Glass Works – X X (on reverse)
Aqua ....$ 6.00— 7.00

Medford Soda Works – Medford, Ore.
Aqua, old crown cap, 8 in. tall ....$ 2.00— 3.00

Montana Bottling Co. – Butte City, Mont.
Aqua, blob top ....$ 8.00—10.00

Matt Mayry – Rudyard, Mich. (all in circle)
Aqua, blob top ....$ 4.00— 6.00

Hippler & Brikson – Telluride, Colo.
Aqua, blob top ....$ 4.00— 6.00

Napa Soda – Phil Caduc – Natural Mineral Water
Cobalt, blob top ....$20.00—25.00

Parkinson & Wise – Yreka
Aqua, 4-piece mold, old crown cap, 7 in. tall ....$ 2.00— 3.00

Red Seal – The Salt Lake City Soda Water Co. (in
embossed seal) – Perfectly Pure (in center of seal)
Same seal on base
Purple, blob top, 6¼ in. tall ....$ 6.00— 9.00

Saxlerner's Bitterquelle – Hunyadi Janos (on base)
Olive green, whittle mold, 9½ in. tall ....$ 6.00— 8.00

Siskiyou Natural Mineral Water – Soda Springs, Ore.
Aqua, beveled base, old crown cap ....$ 3.00— 4.00
Also in brown ....$ 5.00— 8.00

San Francisco Glass Works
Dark blue-green, blob top ....$10.00—12.00

Smith Elmira — N.Y.
Cobalt, whittle mold ....$20.00—25.00

Jos. Steinagher & Son — Yreka, Cal.
Aqua, 4-pc. mold, old crown cap ....$ 2.00— 3.00

Unmarked
Aqua, torpedo-shaped ginger ale ....$18.00—20.00

Owen Casey Eagle Soda Works — Sac. City
Blue-green ....$18.00—20.00

Walter's Napa County Soda — Mineral Water From
Walter's Soda Springs
Aqua, raised horseshoe ....$ 8.00—10.00

Witter Springs Water (around shoulders)
Amber ....$ 3.50— 4.50

Prescott Bottling Works — Prescott, A. T.
Aqua, 8 in. tall, old crown cap ....$ 4.00— 6.00

Ute Chief Mineral Water — Manitou, Colo. — U. T.
(on base)
Purple, 8 in. tall, old crown cap ....$ 3.00— 5.00

Buffalo Lithia Water — Nature's Materia Medica — Trade
Mark — Illus. of lady seated holding pitcher
Aqua, 10 in. tall ....$10.00—12.00

Farmville Lithia Water — Trade Mark Registered —
Illus. of standing figure
Clear, 10 in. tall ....$10.00—12.00

AMETHYSTINE (DESERT GLASS)

This broken, colored glass, its hues altered by the elements to give it something of the appearance of amethyst, has become a popular sideline for the bottle collector. Visiting antique and rock shops, we have seen various ways that amethystine can be used, rare as it is becoming. It can be pieced together into beautiful mosaics, or thick pieces cut and ground into different shapes for bolo ties.

Whiskey necks have been cut and glued onto glass jar liners to be used as toothpick holders and candlesticks. They have also been sliced and made into loop earrings and necklaces. The larger necks make excellent napkin rings or, for the more extravagant, tops may be added by a silversmith to create interesting salt shakers. Let your imagination run free and you may come up with an exciting conversation piece.

INKS

Stafford's Ink
Blue-green, pouring
lip, 10 in. tall
$10.00—12.00

Unmarked
Brown, round, stone bottle;
wide mouth, 7$\frac{1}{2}$ in. tall
$8.50—10.00

Carter's Made in
U.S.A. – Feb. 14,
1899 (patent date,
on base)
Pale green
$7.00—8.00

Unmarked
Tan and white crock, 3 in.
tall
$5.00—6.00

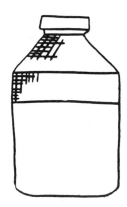

Unmarked
Aqua, beveled
shoulders, square,
small
$2.50—3.00

Sanford Mfg. Co. (on base)
Aqua, sheared lip, 2½
in. tall
$3.00—3.50

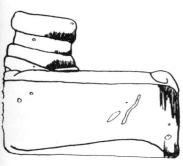

Sanford No. 5,
Patented Nov. 17,
1891 & Nov. 22,
1892 (all on base)
Aqua, shoe shape
$6.00—8.00

Cal. – Ink – Co. – S. F.
(embossed on four sides
of roof)
Red-amber, schoolhouse
ink, square; Rare!
$350.00—500.00

* * *

Schoolhouse inks are scarce items. Besides the red amber illustrated, they may come in light and dark aquas.

The embossed red-amber dates from the late 1880s or 1890. (The California Ink Co. was incorporated in San Francisco in 1891.) The old aquas sold for $40.00 only a few years ago, but are now valued at around $150.00.

INKS NOT ILLUSTRATED

Vitreous Stone Bottles — J. Bourne & Son, Patentees,
Denby Pottery, Near Derby — P. & J. Arnold, London,
England
    Brown, round, with pouring lip ....$ 6.00— 8.00

Unmarked
    White, round pottery; pouring lip; 9 in. tall ....$10.00—12.00

S. S. Stafford's Inks — Made in U.S.A.
    Cobalt, pouring lip, 9½ in. tall ....$10.00—12.00

Unmarked
    Pale ice-green; umbrella inks ....$ 6.00— 8.00

MISCELLANEOUS

Moutarde–Diaphane – Louit
Freres & Co.
Barrel Mustard
$1.00—1.50

Tillman's Extract
Purple, 7½ in. tall
$2.00—2.50

Lea & Perrins Worcestershire
Sauce – A.C.B. Co. (on base)
(This is the older one.)
Green, applied top
$1.25—1.50

Peppersauce
6 panels
Purple
$8.00—10.00

Unmarked (Peppersauce)
12 rings with flat space
for label
Purple, 6-sided
$10.00—12.00

Unmarked (Peppersauce)
8 small, rounded panels;
double ring around neck.
Blue-green; added top
above rings is darker color;
8 in. tall
$15.00—18.00

Unmarked (pickle)
Whittle mold, crudely
added top; bubbly;
open pontil
Ice green
$8.00—10.00

Unmarked (pickle)
Ice green, fluted neck, 9
in. tall
$5.00—6.00

Unmarked (Peppersauce)
Purple, 16 rings, arched
panel, square
$10.00—12.00

Unmarked (catsup)
Purple, 14 panels, pewter
cap
$1.50—2.00

Unmarked (Pickle or relish)
Purple, tapers from base to shoulders, round
$4.00—6.00

Crane Extract Co.
Crane is in raised relief
Purple, 8 in. tall
$4.50—5.00

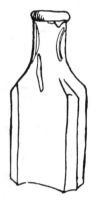

Unmarked (label shows Cayenne Pepper)
Aqua; front and back round inward; rolled lip
$2.00—2.50

Unmarked (pickle)
Aqua, square, various sizes
$2.00—3.00

Unmarked (capers)
Body has 8 indented panels; 10 indented panels on neck; Some have sheared lip
Emerald green, 6½ in. tall
$8.50—10.00

Unmarked (Bordeaux Olive Oils)
Very slim and graceful; bulbous neck
Aqua; three sizes: 7¼ in., 10¼ in., 12¼ in. tall
$3.00—5.00
set **$12.00**

Hunt's Pickles
Purple, round, 6 in.
tall
$2.00—4.00

Peculiar – Heussy & Filz –
Seattle
Aqua, rectangular, 7½
in. tall
$4.00—6.00

Solon Palmer Perfumer
"Palmer green," 4¼
in. tall
$8.00—10.00

Palmer (in biased script)
Blue-green, 5½ and 7 in. tall
$6.50—8.00

Unmarked (perfume)
Triangular glass
stopper
Purple
$3.50—5.00

Unmarked (perfume)
Embossed dragon flies on
shoulders
Purple
$1.50—2.00

Lubin Parfumeur –
Paris
Inside of neck
ground for glass
stopper
Purple, 3¾ in.
tall
$2.50—3.00

Unmarked (Cupie Doll
Perfume)
Metal, crown stopper,
bisque
$10.00—12.00

Unmarked (Cathedral pickle
bottle
Aqua (also in clear); square;
various sizes
$20.00—40.00

MISCELLANEOUS NOT ILLUSTRATED

Armour's Salad Oil
  Green, square, 11½ in. tall .... $ 1.50— 2.00

Mistletoe Salad Oil – National Packing Co., U.S.A.
  Green, square, 11 in. tall .... $ 1.50— 2.00

Preston of New Hampshire
  Blue-green, with matching glass stopper (metal cap
  screws over stopper); square, 3¼ in. tall .... $ 8.00—10.00

The Sherwin Williams Co. (in a circle) — Paint &
Varnish Makers
   (within the circle) .... $ 4.00— 5.00

Unmarked (Barrel Mustard)
   Purple, 3 in. tall .... $ 1.00— 1.50

My Wife's Salad Dressing
   Purple, swirled fluting around neck .... $ 3.00— 4.00

Parker's Hair Balsam (on side panels)
   Brown, rectangular .... $ 2.00— 3.00

Paris Injection Brou — 102 Rue Richlieu
   Purple, 8 panels .... $ 4.00— 5.00

Unmarked (peppersauce)
   Aqua and clear, cathedral shape .... $18.00—25.00

Florida Water — S
   Purple, 7 in. tall .... $ 2.00— 3.00

Murray & Lanman — Druggists — New York — Florida Water
   Aqua, 9 in. tall .... $ 2.50— 3.00

Hoyt's German Cologne — E. W. Hoyt & Co., Lowell, Mass.
   (in sunken panel) .... $ 1.00— 1.50

Bixby — S. M. & Co. — Patented Mch. 6/83
(Initials and patent date on base)
   Aqua; shoe polish .... $ 1.00— 1.50

F. Brown's Ess of Jamaica Ginger — Philada.
   Aqua, 7 in. tall .... $ 4.00— 6.00

Camp Minnow Trap (on front) — Checotah, Okla., Pat.
Pend. (on reverse)
   Aqua, round, 3-pc. whittle mold; $10\frac{1}{2}$ in. tall, 6 in.
   across base; heavy threads on lip, with ground top; in
   each of the mold sections is funnel-shaped hole sunk
   into the bottle; holes are $2\frac{3}{4}$ in. on outside, tapering to
   1 in. on inside; applied top; Heavy mold seams .... $12.00—15.00

Cream of Fresh Lemons — Made by Central Mfg. Co.,
Iowa City, Iowa
Purple, 5 in. tall .... $ 1.00— 1.50

J. W. Hunnewell & Co. — Boston
Aqua, wide mouth, concave sides .... $ 3.50— 4.00

Prof. I. Hubert's Malvina Lotion — Toledo, Ohio
Cobalt, square, 5 in. tall .... $ 6.00— 8.00
Same as above, but in white milk glass .... $ 6.00— 8.00

Langley & Michaels Ess of Jamaica Ginger
Blue-green, whittle mold, bubbly, 5½ in. tall .... $ 4.00— 6.00

Holbrook & Co. (vertically on bottle, also on glass stopper)
Much the same as Lea & Perrins, both in shape and
variety of sizes; 7½ in. tall .... $ 3.00— 3.50

Wisdom's Robertine (on indented front panel)
Paper label shows lady holding hand mirror, peacock on
perch: "A Fluid Face Powder."
Cobalt, rectangular, 5 in. tall .... $ 6.00— 8.00

Colgate Perfume
Purple, 5½ in. tall .... $ 2.00— 2.50

Pagliano — Girolamo
Aqua, square, 4 in. tall .... $ 1.50— 2.00

Excelsior Feeder
Aqua nursing bottle .... $10.00—12.00

Unmarked (champagne girl half-reclining in a goblet
whose base is surrounded with fruit)
China, 4½ in. tall .... $10.00—12.00

Unmarked (lady held in a hand; "A Present For You"
around base) .... $10.00—12.00

Unmarked (Pretzel bottle)
Ceramic .... $ 6.00— 7.00

Unmarked (tamale bottle)
ceramic .... $ 6.00— 7.00

Unmarked (pressed glass horn of plenty)
  Clear, 8 in. tall .... $10.00—12.00

Unmarked (violin bottle)
  Green, 10 in. tall .... $ 5.00— 6.00

Unmarked (fish-shaped cod liver oil)
  Amber, 10 in. tall .... $ 8.00—10.00

Parfumeria Calibri (above and below flying bird
with topknot). Stopper has same bird on top;
sunburst pattern on base
  Blue-green, 5½ in. tall .... $ 6.00— 8.00

Poison (on 2 of 6 panels—3 panels are ribbed)
  Green, also cobalt; 5½ in. tall .... $ 8.00—10.00

Raymond's Complexion Cream – W. T. Co. (on base)
  White milk glass, 5 in. tall .... $ 6.00— 8.00

Dr. Vanderpool's – S. B. – Cough & Consumption Cure
(on front panel) – W. T. Co. (on base)
  Aqua, rectangular, 6¼ in. tall .... $ 2.50— 3.50

Pierre Viau's Pure Sap
  Purple, square, 5 in. tall .... $ 3.00— 4.00

Unmarked (peppersauce)
  Brilliant blue-green, 20 rings, 8½ in. tall .... $18.00—20.00

L. Rose & Co. (heavily embossed with limes and leaves)
  Aqua, 14 in. tall .... $ 6.00— 9.00

Tomato Ketchup – Pittsburgh, U.S.A. (beneath embossed
pickle with "Heinz" on it). Four rows of embossing
make bottle appear squared
  9 in. tall .... $ 2.00— 3.00

Poison (vertically on two panels. Rounded back
panel, dots on three corners, diamond-shaped base
  Amber, 3 in. tall .... $ 3.00— 5.00

E. G. Lyons & Co. Ess Jamaica Ginger – S. F.
  Aqua, 6¼ in. tall .... $ 4.00— 6.00

Prussian Spavin Remedy (in curved front panel)
  Purple, round, 6 in. tall ....$ 4.00— 5.00

Hood's Sarsaparilla (in three small panels) — Apothecaries
C. I. Hood & Co. (on back panel) — Lowell, Mass. (on sides)
  Aqua, 9 in. tall ....$ 3.00— 3.50

C. Heimstreet & Co., Troy, N.Y.
  Cobalt, open pontil, 8-sided, crudely applied lip,
  7 in. tall ....$20.00—30.00

BOTTLE HUNTER'S DREAM

Mileage means nothing to an avid collector who hears of bottles being found. So when Kay and Bettie Lambson of Mexican Hat, Utah, wrote asking us to join them in Colorado, we accepted and asked our friend Blossom Flury to come with us.

Leaving Oregon by the Winnemucca-to-the-sea highway, we traveled across the high desert plateau region. The largest remaining herds of wild antelope in North America roam these plains. Topping one of the plateaus, we surprised a small herd of these fleet-footed, curious, yet shy animals. Coyotes, sage hens, and an occasional bobcat are also often encountered on this route.

Two-and-a-half days after leaving home we reached our destination. A base camp was set up beneath the shelter of pines and spruce at the foot of the Rocky Mountains. We wondered how the altitude would affect our digging, since the smallest camp chore left us breathless.

The following morning Kay took us by Jeep up to an old mine. The narrow, winding road offered spectacular scenery with deep canyons on the left and sheer cliffs rising on the right. Kay was an excellent driver, but we were all relieved when we reached the top. Getting out of the Jeep at the mine, we were chilled by a cold wind racing across the unsheltered summit. The ashen boards of the partially fallen buildings and the starkness of this scene above the timberline, where the sheltered canyons held snow patches from other seasons, awed us.

The former residents of the camp had thrown their empties over the edge of the mine tailings, which made our work considerably easy: We would merely have to dig the bottles out of the side of the bank.

Several times that day the Jeep gave us shelter from the cold drizzle of low-hanging clouds. Between showers, we unearthed some excellent bottles: a beautifully embossed Quaker Maid whiskey flask, some of the old medicines with their boastful labels, and many iridescent wines and beers. On a previous visit Kay had found a dark olive green bottle, fifteen inches tall, with a long, bulbous neck. Around the shoulders in heavy, ornate script was **Amara di Felsina G. Buton & G.** Although we had hoped to match that find, our searching proved fruitless. Satisfied at last with the bottles we had, we began the descent which, for our excitement, seemed less arduous than the climb.

The next morning we hurried through breakfast and drove in to pick up Kay. The area he had chosen for the day's hunt was inaccessible by car; we drove as far as we could and walked the remaining two miles on foot. The trail was narrow, rocky, and steep and the saddle toward which we headed lay high above us. Our rest stops increased in frequency the higher we climbed. On one of those occasions we watched the tiny cony, or rock rabbit, busily gathering grass and stacking it to dry for the long winter. He resembles a young rabbit without the characteristic rabbit ears. His bleeping call followed us up the mountainside.

Arriving at the top, elevation 12,700 feet, we were rewarded with a panoramic view. We stood a moment trying to envision the trips made over that tortuous trail by the early day miner, the long strings of pack mules loaded with supplies, their harness straps jingling as they plodded up the mountain, and their return trips loaded down with high grade ore.

Farther along the trail could be seen old, dilapidated buildings, the bottle hunter's dream. And in the center of the basin, which holds a record for production with ore assays that ran up to 900 ounces to the ton, lay a small lake with three abandoned mines around its shore.

We soon had our own mining operation under way, digging out a Kennedy's Medical Discovery, a Paine's Celery Compound, a Tonico Bitters, and a Quaker Maid Whiskey in the flask and also in the round quart size. We found many clear, coffin-shaped flasks as well as the half-pint ones with short, bulbous necks. The olive green of the whittle mold Ferro China Bisleri and the lovely rainbow hues of the iridescent inks and pickles were joys to behold. The most interesting bottle of all was a clear, horseshoe-shaped flask with a sheared lip and a rough base. Its only decoration were the initials "G.D." on one side. Appearing older than the other bottles, it might have been some miner's personal flask, possibly a gift, that had been carried for many years from one boom camp to another.

We could take only a few of the choice bottles with us, since they had to be packed two miles to the car. The rumble of thunder from approaching black clouds signaled a storm. So after hurriedly packing the chosen bottles, we began our descent down the mountain.

Dislodged rocks sounded like small avalanches as their rattling noise echoed across the canyon. To this the wee cony piped his anxiety over the advancing storm. Our party reached the car only minutes ahead of the cold, pelting rain. As we took a last look at the saddle, we agreed that our efforts had not really touched the wealth of bottles still there, which we intend to prove on our next trip to our "bottle mine" in Colorado.

Bottle hunters on a rough trail high in the Colorado Rockies

Destination of hunters: abandoned mining camp, elevation 12,700 feet.
Frequent storms occur at this altitude, even in summer.

Bettie and Kay Lambson of Mexican Hat, Utah, with a beautiful olive green bottle, 15 inches tall, a 36 cal. cap and ball pistol, and a whiskey decanter with stopper.

Setting up a goody—Gilka

Typical miners' cabins which produce whiskeys, medicines and coins

In the pay streak, left to right: Pottery ink; crock jug; benedictine; tall, blue-green turn mold wine; black 3-piece mold; green capers.

Deep aqua Ernst L. Arp – Kiel pepsin bitters. There is a gold eagle embossed on the green wine bottle.

BOTTLES AND RELICS

The bottle hunter of today is experiencing the same thrill the early day prospector felt on discovering a promising mineral outcrop. No matter whether it is in an antique shop, a junk shop, or a dump behind a decaying cabin, the excitement of making the "find" is the same.

Research in old atlases and topographical maps may help to pinpoint locations of the abandoned homesteads and old mines that dot the West. And a metal detector may be invaluable for revealing the dumps that have sodded over. Old railroad lines often aid in locating homesteads whose land was once used for access roads. At one such location, our party of nine unearthed some 125 choice bottles covering a range of bottled goods.

While searching for bottles, other relics should not be overlooked, however. Mrs. Blanche Sublette of Red Bluff, California, found an 1871 C. C. mint dime while digging for bottles in Virginia City, Nevada. This coin is very rare and worth a high price from a collector.

The author's neighbor, Mert Thomson, found an octagon-barrel pistol, an old rifle, and a number of iron pots with squat legs—all while on bottle hunts! A man skilled in tracing lost sites, Mert uncovered Chinese opium pipe bowls, a quantity of other Chinese artifacts, and an 1881 five-dollar gold piece largely while searching out the early railroad camps, which often appear as flat, terraced areas along streams and adjacent to the rail beds.

Bottle collecting is a fascinating and rewarding hobby in itself; yet if one will widen his sights in his explorations, the rewards can be all the greater.

Mert Thomson of Eagle Point, Oregon, with his bottles and relics

Left to right: amber cone ink, Cobalt Laxol, Dr. Walker's V. B. (Vinegar Bitters), yellow green whiskey, early day miner's candle holder.

A treasure from Treasure City—"lady's leg"

A few sagebrush finds

Lustrous beauties silhouetted against a ruin of the 1860s

The authors with part of their flask collection, dating from the 1860s

Frontier relics found while searching for bottles

ORIENTAL ARTIFACTS

CHINESE BOTTLES

During the gold rush of '49, thousands of Chinese made their way from the Orient to San Francisco and out into the gold fields. Mistreated by the white miners and subjected to ridicule, they were fre quently driven from their own claims and forced to work the tailings. But being diligent miners and working long hours, they were still able to realize substantial returns.

Their chief enjoyment after a hard day was the delirium of opium smoking. This narcotic came in brass or copper cans similar to the "cut plug" tobacco cans, and in a variety of other sizes. It is said that well-to-do miners paid up to $100.00 for them. The opium can is most often found along with soy sauce bottles, gin jugs, and the tiny, sheared lip medicine bottles. The last have been dubbed "opiums" by collectors, but it is doubtful that they ever contained the dark brown, gummy substance; it would have been extremely difficult to extract opium from the type. These "opiums" are extraordinarily fragile and have been known to disintegrate upon handling.

Chinese characters on front
Cobalt, tiny dragon on
neck, 2 in. tall
$15.00—18.00

Unmarked
Aqua, plain, sheared
lip, 3 in. tall;
uneven, round
$2.50—3.00

Unmarked (soy sauce)
Jug with tiny pouring spout,
flared lip
$4.00—5.00

Purple, round, Chinese
writing on base
$3.50—4.00

Round, Chinese writing
on sides, 3 in. tall
$4.00—5.00

Chinese medicine bottle,
referred to as "opium"
Various shades of green,
tiny, square, sheared lip,
full of minute bubbles, 2 to
2½ in. tall
$1.00—1.50

ORIENTAL RELICS

Cumberland, British Columbia, on Vancouver Island has been a collector's paradise for oriental collectables. The old buildings have been torn down and burned, one by one, as the last of the Chinese residents died or moved away. Most of the following items are mementoes from that area, although similar bottles have been found in most of the old mining camps.

Information on the contents of some of the containers and the uses for many of the items was gathered from the Chinese still living there.

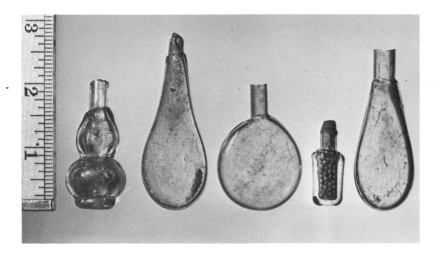

Prized by collectors, these tiny bottles once contained medicines, either small pills, powders, or liquid, which were reputed to cure a wide range of discomforts, and might have been prescribed for external or internal use, or both.

The double bulb is quite rare. The large teardrop dispensed fluid a drop at a time (a smaller teardrop held a powder similar to boric acid and was used to soothe sore eyes). The third bottle from the left is said to be "banjo-shaped." The small square bottle contains its original pills.

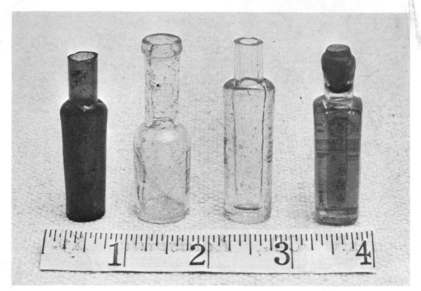

Left to right: A dark emerald green with sheared lip; a long-necked clear, with embossing on the neck; an oval-shaped bottle in aqua with sheared lip; and the most common of all the "opium bottles." This one is still filled with the original medicine. The label claims it is effective against skin disease and seasickness.

Left to right: The clear square bottle is embossed on one side with "Tiensautong Hong Kong." The light cobalt blue, six-sided bottle was a poison. Three of its sides are vertically ribbed, and one is embossed with Chinese characters.

Inks: Square, sheared lip, cobalt blue; aqua, sheared lip, eight sides

The wooden domino-like blocks belong to a game called PI QUE. The little Peking glass button-like items came in colors of blue, white, and green, and were used in a gambling game, FAN TAN, in which the buttons are maneuvered beneath a cup and their positions bet upon. The metal discs are Chinese money.

These small brown glazed jars came in three known sizes and
held sweets, salves, cosmetics, and spices.

Two keys and a lock

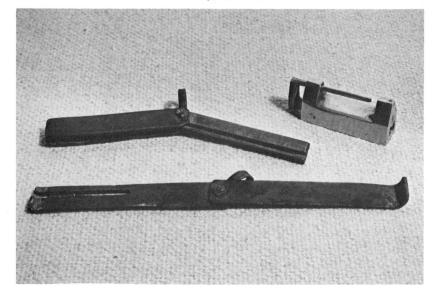

Opium-pipe bowls came in several interesting shapes and a wide
variety of colors. The bowls were fitted onto a pipestem.

Opium lamps or burners: The bases are of pewter with a hand-rotated draft. Sitting
on the bases are small glass peanut oil fuel containers cut and etched in both blue
and cranberry, with a matching washer-type disc on top. Covering the fuel cups
are ornately etched clear glass domes. The opium bowls were held over the hole in
the top of the dome to heat the narcotic. These two lamps are from a cache of
several that were uncovered on Vancouver Island.

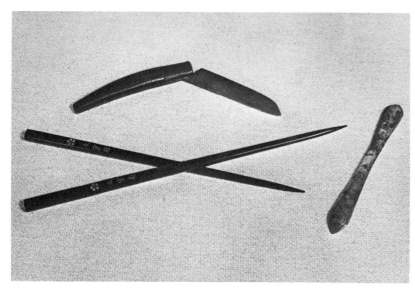

The pointed ebony sticks resembling chopsticks and the engraved metal piece were used by the Chinese women as hair ornaments. The knife was for cutting hair.

The small, hand-painted pitcher held saki or other liquor, and the toy-sized china bowls are "shot glasses."

These are old ginger pots. (The modern version is six-sided rather than round.) They are most frequently green, with sometimes a mottled glaze. The china spoons have been found in a variety of fancy designs and colors.

These bowls with unglazed bases are mortars for grinding ink blocks. The small brass boxes contain a pasty ink to be used with an ink stick, an implement similar to chopsticks but shorter.

The smaller of the handleless cups was used for sauce, the larger for tea. Also pictured are two small plates.

Old rice or soup bowls

The small, clear, six-sided glass jar has a tiger embossed both on the base and on one side, signifying it as a container for Tiger Balm. The larger jar is sun-colored amethystine and has a zinc lid. This jar is embossed on each of three sides with Chinese characters and a bird; on the fourth side with: Chan Moon Kee — Rose Bean Curd — Made in China — Hong Kong.

These three slim, bubbly bottles held a Chinese florida water. Paper labels have revealed a "his" and "her" brand.

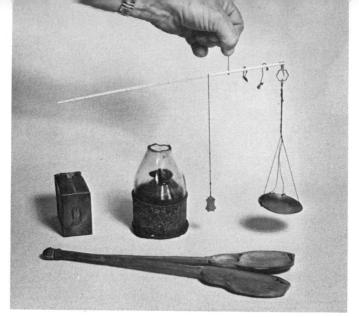

This opium lamp is home-made, utilizing a tin can for the base, an ink bottle for the peanut oil fuel container, and a broken bottle for the dome. The brass boxes are common in all the old Chinese camps and held tea or opium. The hand holds Chinese gold-and-opium scales, below which lies their violin-shaped container.

The two long pipes have brass bowls and mouthpieces, and supposedly held tobacco. The other pipe IS a tobacco pipe. The item with the long spout is a lamp; the spout held the wick.

These jugs came in a variety of glazed colors and are commonly referred to as "Tiger Whiskies," although some held whiskey and others a medicinal wine.

Most collectors have one of these soy sauce pots, recognizable by their tiny spouts

This square pot with the tiny spout was also a container for soy sauce, but a rare variation which has been found almost exclusively on Vancouver Island.

This double-handled metal cooking utensil, called a Wok, was an excellent vegetable cooker. The metal ladle was used to stir and serve the cooked food.

This long-handled pot served, among other uses, as a noodle cooker; the wire sieve as a noodle strainer.

Good representatives of relics from Cumberland, a coal mining town on Vancouver Island—a saw and an ancient miner's pick.

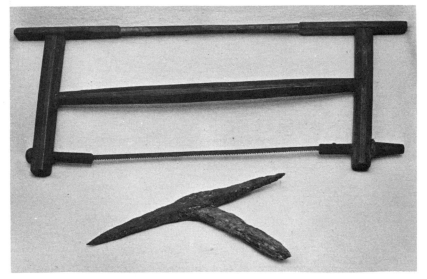

This wooden contrivance resembling a doll's crib is a neckrest for sleeping that prevented the elegant coiffure of the oriental woman from being disturbed. The wood was originally padded with material which has long since rotted away.

These small, fancy, hand-painted platters were used to serve roast duck or chicken, or fruit and candy.

This heavily ornamented brass vase is, in reality, a cooker similar to a hibachi. Coals were put inside the container and the cooking vessel was set on top. It could be used right at the table.

Bottles from many parts of the world have been excavated at Cumberland, B.C.
San Miguel Brewery — Manila, P.I.; olive green, blob top
Original Abzug — Schutz — Marke (on either side of angelic figure holding a stein, which is above the monogram "A.B.") — Eigenthum der Actien — Bierbrauerei — Hamburg St. Pauli (on reverse); green, blob top.
Original Abzug — Schutz — Marke (on either side of embossed bear whose front feet rest on a castle shield) — Brauerei Bahrenfeld (below castle); golden amber, slightly bulged neck. The last two are German beers.

Left to right: Rice wine bottle: Dark green, ring-necked, older press cap. These also came in olive green and amber, embossed with "Wing Lee Wai."

Chinese bitters: Amber, somewhat squat, slight kick-up base. Inside the flat seal on the shoulder is embossed face of a dragon or a mask.

Rice wine bottle: A beautiful blue-green with a ring neck. This color is popular with collectors, especially for a window display. Others are crudely made in various shades of blues, greens, and a rare yellow.

RECOMMENDED BOOKS

OLD BOTTLES AND GHOST TOWNS
$2.15

BOTTLE TALK
Adele Reed
272 Shepard Lane
Bishop, California
$2.15

THE BOTTLE TRAIL
May Jones
Box 23
Nara Visa, N.M.
6 volumes @ **$1.65** each

A BOTTLE COLLECTOR'S BOOK
Bob and Pat Ferraro
Box 239
Lovelock, Nevada 89419
$3.25

THE PAST IN GLASS
Bob and Pat Ferraro
$3.25

PERIODICALS

NATIONAL BOTTLE GAZETTE
John Fountain, Editor
Amador City, California
$5.00/year

OLD BOTTLE MAGAZINE
Box 243
Bend, Oregon
(monthly—**$5.00**/year)

WESTERN COLLECTOR
P.O. Box 9166
San Francisco, California
(monthly—**50c**/copy; **$5.00**/year)

PARTIAL LIST OF BOTTLE SHOPS

ARIZONA
  Apache Junction
    Frederich's Rock Ranch
  Ashfork
    Winnie's Rock Shop
  Phoenix
    Antique Outpost
    Ogilby Gold Rock Ranch
  Quartzsite
    Chas. Oldham
    Ghost Town Jewelry
  Wickenburg
    A.B.C. Shop

CALIFORNIA
  Amador City
    Amador City Antiques &
      Bottles
    The Glass Bottle
  Argus
    Searles Valley Rock Shop
  Blythe
    Southwestern Antiques
  Boron
    Hazel's Old Dish Shop
  Compton
    Compton Rock Shop
  Fort Jones
    Coor's Carriage House
  Mohave
    Desert Wind Gift Shop
  Napa
    Barbette Giveables
  Randsburg
    Ghost Town Shop
  Redding
    Olde West Shoppe
  Sonora
    Jewel's Antiques

Tiburon
  Wild West Shop
Yreka
  Corky Dell Antiques

COLORADO
  Colorado Springs
    A.B.C. Antiques
    Levine's
  La Salle
    The Bottle Shop
  Leadville
    Ghost Town Bottles
    Tabor Art & Gifts
  Meeker
    The Garrison

FLORIDA
  Miami
    Trade Winds Antiques
  Pensacola
    Old Time Bottle Shop

IDAHO
  Spalding
    Spalding Rock & Gem

KANSAS
  Haviland
    Ballard's Bottle Barn
  Wichita
    Ebersole Lapidary

MONTANA
  Alder
    Sylvia's Rocking Horse
  Bozeman
    Horse Shoe Inn

Drummond
Ray's Rock Shop
Ennis
The Wayfarer
Virginia City
Vigilante Bottle Shop
Windham
Ivan Zimmer

NEVADA
Battle Mountain
Todd's Rock Shop
Ely
Family Store
Eureka
The Morgue
Reno
West Second Antiques
Virginia City
House of Bottles

OREGON
Baker
Ilah's Antiques
Bandon
Hazel's Antiques
Brookings
Ruby's Tackle
Dexter
The Bottle Tree
Jacksonville
Oregon Trader
Lakeview
Davis Rock Shop

Medford
Nelson's Bottle & Rock
Shop
Duc-Ett's Rock Shop
Newport
Poke-A-Bout
Portland
Taylor's Antiques
Prineville
Prineville Bottle Shop
Prospect
Langley's Antiques
Salem
Old Time Bottle
Publishing Co., Bottle
and Relic Museum
Shaniko
Shaniko Hotel
Tumulo
Tumulo Emporium
Vida
Hawthorne Farms

WASHINGTON
Aberdeen
House of Charles
Chinook
The Bottle Collector,
Howard Johnson
Entiat
William's Lapidary
Grayland
Gray Gull Gift Shop
Seattle
Rohrer's Junk & Antiques

FIND REFERENCE INDEX

This index, divided into two parts, has been designed to facilitate the rapid identification and pricing of a find. If the bottle is etched or embossed with a name or brand, the following regular index should be consulted. Generally, the manufacturer's or bottler's name should be used as a key. But if the embossing consists only of a slogan or a place name, the first significant word in that line should be used. If a label is still attached, it can often be found in this portion of the index.

However, if no writing is evident, and only an embossed or etched picture, a shape, a design, or a color distinguishes the bottle from another, the special DESCRIPTIVE INDEX which follows this regular index must be used.

DESCRIPTIVE INDEX

This index is meant to expedite the identification and pricing of bottles that do not have embossed or etched names. A bottle should be keyed by its most obvious characteristic. Some of the bottles listed are cross-referenced, but only when one characteristic is considered as important as another.

The index proceeds from the most distinguishing qualities to the most general: special sculpted shapes, embossments and etchings, standard shapes, bottle composition, and, finally, color. If a bottle is of a peculiar shape, say, teardrop or fish, refer to the first listing. If it has an embossed picture or design, refer to the next; if a precise number of body panels or rings or a distinctive cut, to the next; if made of a material other than glass, the next. If, however, its only distinguishing characteristic is its color, refer to the color guide. Remember, a fish-shaped aqua bottle will probably be found under SPECIAL SCULPTED SHAPES rather than COLOR, because the fish shape is its most distinctive quality.

White